THE

Education of the People

AND

The Bill of 1902.

PRICE SIXPENCE, or 20s. per 100.

PRINTED AND PUBLISHED BY

P. S. KING & SON, ORCHARD HOUSE, WESTMINSTER,

FOR THE

NATIONAL EDUCATION ASSOCIATION,

SURREY HOUSE, VICTORIA EMBANKMENT, LONDON, W.C.

CONTENTS.

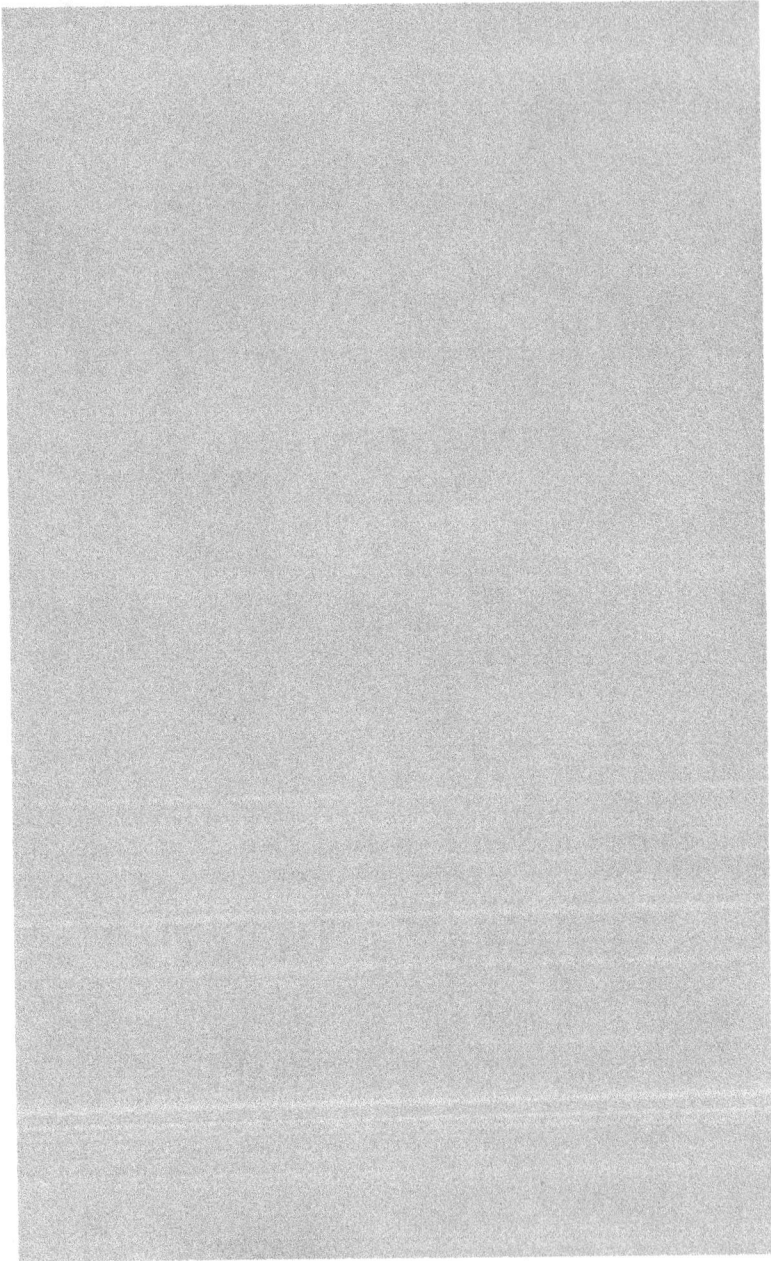

THE EDUCATION OF THE PEOPLE AND THE BILL OF 1902.

CHAPTER I.—PRINCIPLES OF PROGRESS.

MANY streets are brilliantly lighted. Thoughtful and wealthy residents place lamps above their doors; the churches and public buildings are surrounded by their private lights; the tradesman strives by the greater brilliance of his illuminations to fix public attention on his premises. In these ways many thoroughfares are rendered practically independent of public lighting. Yet the lighting of the streets is not made to depend upon such voluntary and haphazard provision. If it were, those places which most require light would be left in the blackest darkness, and even the main thoroughfares would not be always lighted, for these voluntary provisions established for private purposes often cease when the public need is still great. So we have organised a national system of public authorities with the duty, power, and means of providing adequate illumination in each street according to its needs.

In like manner we charge different bodies with the work of meeting the national necessity for good roads, for adequate drainage, and for the supply, to rich and poor alike, of a sufficient quantity of pure water. Measures are taken for the provision of almost every public requirement, the absence of which creates a public evil. This is secured by placing in the hands of those who gain or suffer by these things the power of providing and managing them. They have at command a properly organised machinery of local self-government by which their wants may be met.

A

The National Need.

The national need for the adequate and suitable education of each individual can be supplied only by similar methods. The voluntary agencies that are at work are very numerous, cover an immense amount of ground, and, to the superficial observer, might seem to do all that is required. Philanthropists have endowed grammar schools, colleges, and universities for the rich, and ragged and industrial schools for the poor. On all sides one sees private schools of various types run by good business men, who conduct them efficiently and profitably. The churches have established schools to serve as "bulwarks" of their sectarian organisations, while hundreds of public or semi-public bodies, such as City Guilds, Town and County Councils, and the Gilchrist Trustees do invaluable pieces of work in the educational field. But neither separately nor in the bulk do these give us a national system of education.

Like the persons whose private enterprise aids in the lighting of the streets, these educational agencies are in most cases under no obligation to do anything. Their funds are limited ; their purpose embraces only some narrow portion of the whole field, and upon this they bestow their favours. They may satisfy the educational wants of the individuals whom they select, but they leave many needs untouched. In short, all these different bodies, many of them doing admirable work, have not the first essential of a national system, which is that it shall take cognisance of and be compelled to provide for every individual.

The Essential Elements.

When Parliament determined in 1870 that every child in the nation should receive a certain amount of schooling, it attempted to give statutory form to a scientific conception of what a national educational system must be. As the basis of everything the Act calls for a census to be taken in each district to ascertain the numbers, ages, and standing of all possible scholars. Secondly, full information has to be obtained regarding the existing schools, the mode in which they are managed, the suitability of the premises, the qualifications of the teachers, the instruction given, the fees charged, and many other details. Thirdly, wherever the provision of school places compared with the children of school age shows a deficiency; wherever the wants of any individual, be he even the poorest little street arab, are not already covered—then arrangements must be made forthwith to fill the gap. For this purpose the ratepayers elect a School Board, which has by statute the necessary powers to take land, build schools, and do whatever else is necessary to supply the deficiency. Like the sanitary authority, the police authority, the poor law, and other authorities, this education authority has unlimited rating and borrowing powers, so that its work cannot be hindered for want of funds. In case this body neglects to supply the necessities of a district, the Board of Education has power to appoint officers to do the work, and once these substitutes are nominated, the members of the negligent School Board cease to have any power—in the words of the Act, they are "deemed to have vacated their offices as if they were dead"—and the officers appointed in their place perform all the duties and exercise all the powers of the Board.

This obligation to provide for every available scholar, this power of the unlimited rating and borrowing, with the direct control of the public on one hand, backed by the power of the central government to sweep aside a defaulting local authority, are essential elements in a national system.

SCHOOL MANAGEMENT.

As to the management of the schools, the Act of 1870 laid down most important principles. It provided that every penny expended out of the rates shall be controlled by the representatives of the ratepayers; every school aided from the School Board's funds being exclusively managed by the members or their nominees. This prevents that inevitable waste, inefficiency, and injustice which come when doles and subsidies are given from public funds to private persons to spend almost as they please. Further, the principle that national education shall not be subordinated to the interests of any religious denomination or political party was established, if not made effective in operation. That the religious teaching shall be unsectarian in public schools, and that no child shall be compelled to receive religious instruction against the wish of its parents or guardians, were principles which Parliament sanctioned. Parliament decided that nobody could be excluded from a seat on the education authority by a property disqualification, sex disability, or religious test, the ratepayers being free to elect whoever receives their confidence. All these judicious enactments make not only for progress, but for an education which is sound in all essentials and acceptable to all classes.

LIMITATIONS OF THE ACT OF 1870.

This powerful combination of local and national forces, working upon the basis of a scientfic ascertainment of the needs of every individual, and backed by drastic machinery for supplying all shortcomings, would provide us with a national system of education were it not for certain limitations of the Act of 1870. In estimating the population needing education, that statute took no cognisance of children over thirteen years of age. And it did not inquire into the standing of any school of which the fees are more than ninepence a week, or the quality of the education given in it. These are arbitrary and artificial distinctions. The suitable education of scholars above thirteen years of age is, in many cases, more a matter of national concern than that of younger children; while, if investigation is to be made as to the value of the teaching given in other establishments, it is absurd to allow a school to secure exemption by charging fees above ninepence a week. The only consequence of the latter provision is to consign many children to practically worthless places of instruction; and the consequence of the former is that the mass of children over thirteen are not provided for at all.

THE LINE OF EXTENSION.

To complete a national system it is necessary to apply the principles of 1870 in some form or other to the education of older scholars, and to the schools and colleges which charge high fees. Practically all the turmoil and political dissension which make up "the education question" is caused by the enemies of popular education and the proprietors of various vested interests fighting and intriguing against the application of these simple and successful principles. The public mind is confused by wrangles as to the suitability of clergy or laity, members of School Boards or town councillors, farmers or squires, business men or educational "experts," to provide and administer the educational system. These are minor considerations. All experience of local self-government proves that success does not depend upon particular individuals or corporate bodies, but upon the powers, responsibilities, and obligations with which both the electors and their representatives are endowed. Whoever the persons controlling the work may be, provision must be made for making them sensitive to public requirements, and able to meet them. The advantage of the local authority being under a statutory obligation to provide for every scholar, and of having no statutory limitation to expenditure, is obvious. These provisions remove the incentive to neglect and provide for punishment where indifference creeps in. There are ample checks in the other direction. There is the principle that every member of the education authority must be directly elected by the ratepayers who find the money. He has periodically to face the electors and render an account of his stewardship. Nothing has so strikingly contributed to rapid progress with all possible economy as this popular election, whilst the power to sweep away a defaulting authority is a silent irresistible force ever pressing on the elected representative in the direction of efficiency.

The Act of 1889.

Judged by the principles of progress embodied in the Act of 1870, what are we to think of the Act of 1889 and the Bills of 1896, 1900, and 1901? The Act of 1889 did a little to cover part of the field excluded from the Act of 1870. It enabled County and Borough Councils to provide technical education up to the limit of a penny rate to scholars of any age who were not in attendance at a public elementary school, but nearly all the principles of progress enumerated above were omitted, and the progress made has been in many cases very inadequate. Even the penny rate is seldom levied, and if it had not been for the accidental windfall of a large Government subsidy in the form of the money intended for the buying up of public-house licenses, which has been increasingly used for education by the County Councils, the Act of 1889 would have been a dead letter in many parts of the country. In some places, by setting up a rival authority to the existing School Boards, chaos and friction has been created. The Act of 1889 was forced through Parliament late at night at the fag end of a session practically without discussion.

THE BILLS OF 1896, 1900, 1901, AND 1902.

Since 1889, there have been other Bills, and in these the "principles of progress" have been much more remarkably absent than in the Act of 1889. The only good feature of these Bills was that they met to a certain extent the needs of those scholars who are not provided for by the Act of 1870. The bad features were many, and may be briefly enumerated :—

(1) The abolition of the present powers of County and Urban Councils, the ultimate abolition of School Boards, and the creation of a new authority, removed as far as possible from the influence of the electorate who have to gain or suffer by their work.

(2) No obligation to provide suitable schools, nor any power to secure suitability as regards fees, staff, or curriculum in existing schools.

(3) The absence of the statutory requirement, on pain of extinction, to provide sufficient school accommodation and efficient instruction for every available scholar not otherwise suitably provided for.

(4) An extension of the old system of subsidising schools under private and sectarian management, which has always proved to be an extravagant and inefficient manner of spending public money.

(5) No absolute control over any funds whatever, the authority being dependent on doles from the Government or the local municipal bodies or on the gifts of philanthropists.

(6) A large proportion of the members to be appointed by sectarian and professional organisations and other vested interests, a number not less than a majority to be nominated by the municipal councils, none directly elected by the public, and no security for any freedom in selection, exclusive tests on the ground of sex, residence, property, religion, &c., being inevitable in many cases and probable in others.

(7) The Bill of 1902 pretends that the Council of each county and of the larger boroughs will decide the constitution

of the new authority, but it only enables them to "draft schemes," and it enables the Board of Education to reject these schemes and proceed to make other schemes of its own.

It is obvious from this brief summary that in framing the constitution of the authority, in endowing it with an income, in the providing of schools, or increasing the efficiency of education, all the initiatory and compelling forces which make for progress are absent or restricted, and the last word is in all cases left with whatever obstructive forces may arise.

Quietly and insidiously the principles of progress which have stood the test of thirty years' daily application are either ignored or swept aside. Yet these things, which the present Government endeavours to break down, are the foundations upon which any really national system of education must be built. In every other department of local self-government most of these selfsame principles have worked well under the severest strain. They have been applied to the provision of gas, water, drains, poor relief, and endless other communal needs. None but the enemies of popular progress would even argue that they can with advantage be excluded from the field of national education.

CHAPTER II.—PRINCIPLES OF REACTION.

HAVING reviewed certain of the principles which make for progress, let us briefly consider the influences which hinder advance. Much of the obstruction is grounded in nothing more than prejudice, selfishness, and meanness, but it would be unwise to deny the title of "principle" to the theory that the education of the lower classes is contrary to the well-being of the community. The vague notion that "men and women were much better servants when they could neither read nor write" is firmly held by persons who honestly believe that in acting upon that maxim they are working for the public good. Many persons possess no other firm conviction upon the subject of national education, and in Parliament this mistaken idea is unceasingly operative.

THE CLERICAL CONSPIRACY.

Another principle which has been an even stronger prop to the cause of reaction is expressed in the words, " The education of the country should be under the control and auspices of the Established Church." These words, spoken by an Archbishop of Canterbury in 1807, served to destroy the Education Bill of that year, and the policy which they tersely summarised has killed or mutilated every effort at reform throughout the century that has followed. The struggle between "popular control" and "clerical control" is not peculiar to England; it has been fought, or is being fought, in every civilised land. To those who do not go deeply into "the principles of things," the churches may seem to be suitable bodies to control education. The clergy have obvious qualifications. When made directly responsible to public opinion through popular election, involving as it does the probability of popular rejection if proved unworthy, clergymen are most suitable members of School Boards and other elected bodies. Experience proves, however, that no body of men, not even the clergy, is efficient when entrusted with absolute power. Where the duties of the State are delegated to religious organisations, the inevitable conflict between public duty and sectarian loyalty too often ends in injury to the public interest.

SECTARIAN PROPAGANDA.

The present Archbishop of Canterbury told the Royal Commission of 1860 that the zeal which religious leaders show in promoting education always takes the direction of advancing their own religious opinions, and that in place of a sense of public duty, or philanthropy, or patriotism, there is a predominant desire to use the schools in order to extend the influence of a particular denomination. He said further that this sectarian propagandism is a quiet element when it has its own way, but if any attempt is made to thwart it, strife and discord follow. In that warning one discovers the key of the "strife and discord" which has marked an entire century of educational debate. The determination of the clergy to pursue this sectarian propaganda in the schools is the dominant factor in the struggle and chaos of to-day.

Lord Hugh Cecil objects to the phrase "clerical conspiracy." He thinks a conspiracy must be something secret and sinister, but he and his friends pursue their ideals in the full light of day, and are satisfied in their own consciences that their aims are pure and noble. Sincere religious proselytism is, no doubt, worthy of respect from one point of view, but it is most intolerable from another. In Germany, Luther; in Scotland, John Knox; and in America, the Pilgrim Fathers taught those nations that they must cry "hands off" to either priest or laymen who would use the public schools for private and sectarian purposes, and the national systems of education which have grown up in those countries under popular control are the envy, admiration, and despair of English reformers to-day.

CLERICAL IDEALS.

With all respect, therefore, for the character and aims of the "conspirators," let us attempt some review of the prolonged struggle with the conspiracy. A century of strife has clearly proved that the ideas of "clerical control" are— (1) That all scholars of all denominations shall be compelled to attend schools in which "the first and chief thing taught" is "the national religion according to the excellent liturgy and catechism provided by our Church"; (2) that the scholars shall be compelled to receive this instruction and to attend Church and Sunday School; (3) that no one shall be a teacher who is not a communicant of the Established Church; (4) that there shall be a like test for managers, coupled with a high property qualification; (5) that the appointment and dismissal of teachers and the ultimate control of the schools shall be vested in the clergy, with no appeal except to the Bishop.

Broadly speaking, the majority of our elementary schools, most of the public schools and colleges are founded upon this basis, although a distinction may be drawn between the different churches. The Roman Catholics, the Jews, and occasionally other denominations ask only for special schools for the use of their co-religionists, whereas the full claim of the Established Church of England is to control the education of the whole nation. This broad difference is sometimes obscured by the fact that high-minded Anglicans shrink from the full application of the obligations to be found in their trust deeds.

Incidentally, although not necessarily, the clericals have

opposed real developments, identifying themselves with the theory that the most suitable education for the mass of the people is that which "renders them patient, humble, and moral, and relieves the hardship of their present lives by the prospect of a bright eternity."

Throughout the long space of years from 1807 to 1870 the clericals had the upper hand. They defeated the reformers, and secured the rejection of all legislation; they captured the central government, and they obtained a monopoly of elementary education in most districts, leaving other people no option but to assist in maintaining schools established upon principles which they abhorred, or to abstain from the work of promoting education.

THE ATTACK ON THE SCHOOL BOARDS.

At last the Act of 1870 checked the clerical propaganda, the scholars in their schools were given a statutory exemption from sectarian tests; but the teachers and managers were left subject to these, so that reform of the existing schools was not thorough. However, the Act of 1870 also created public authorities (School Boards) on a democratic basis, and gave them power to open schools which should be free, unsectarian, under popular control, and made efficient at the expense of the rates. Thus the principle of "clerical control" was confronted by the principle of "popular control." As a consequence, the School Board system immediately became the object of the bitter antagonism of the clerical party, and all the forces of reaction have been concentrated on measures to cripple or destroy it. The first aim was to prevent competition, and in 1873 the Marquis of Salisbury forced an alteration in the law which made the right of the School Boards to build schools—given by the Act of 1870—to depend on the will of the Education Department.

ATTENDANCE COMMITTEES.

In 1876 he legalised the abolition of School Boards, and provided a new form of education authority—"School Attendance Committees"—to take their place wherever they were abolished or had not been created. These Committees are not directly elected, they are appointed by Town Councils or Boards of Guardians, they have no power to provide schools under any circumstances or to secure efficiency in existing schools, and their only educational function is to compel the attendance of the children at the existing schools. The Act of 1876 also contained a provision relieving the managers of Clerical Schools from the obligation to provide at least half of the ordinary expenses of maintaining their schools which had been imposed in 1870. Since then the Parliamentary Grant has been increased again and again—by the Fee Grant (1891), the Aid Grant (1897), the Block Grant (1899), and by the many changes in the Code—until in practice it has become possible for the Clerical Schools to be entirely maintained by public money. Superficially this covering of the country with School Attendance Committees on an elected basis might appear to be a concession to the principle of popular control; in reality it outflanked the School Board system.

Technical Instruction Committees.

This outflanking policy was developed in 1889 by the creation of similar Committees to take the work of technical education out of the purview of the School Boards. These bodies also, like the School Attendance Committees, are not directly elected by the ratepayers, they may meet in secret; their resources were strictly limited to the produce of a penny rate, although the whiskey money has now been added; their educational powers are restricted; they are under no statutory obligation to do anything, and, unlike the School Boards, they can give subsidies to clerical and other schools not under their own management, and they often spend their money in subsidising Clerical Schools. These Committees can admit any number of members, not elected by the public, to practically equal power with the elected members. The establishment of these Committees is permissive, and the Bill sanctioning them was forced through Parliament under the auspices of the extreme clerical party almost without debate in the last hours of a protracted session.

Diocesan Associations.

In 1897 an Act dictated by the extreme clerical party was passed which enabled the whole country to be divided into ecclesiastical districts, and powerful Diocesan Associations have been established in each. These are allowed to administer part of the Government Grant, thus giving them an effective voice in the management of the schools. Thus, whilst the system of "popular control" has been effectively crippled and thrown into a chaos of conflicting authorities, areas, and powers, a system of "clerical control" of national scope has been quietly built up. All these things have been done without the real knowledge or consent of Parliament.

COCKERTON.

Then outside Parliament the clerical party, assisted by the Government, has recently been successful in promoting the Cockerton case, and in obtaining an interpretation of the law which restricts School Boards to the "elementary" education of "children," thereby making most of the Higher Grade work and the Evening Schools under popular control illegal. The clerical evening schools are untouched by the judgment, and the Government have further aided them by sweeping away most of the statutory restrictions placed upon the Clerical Schools in 1870, such as the conscience clause, the limitation of fees, the audit of accounts, the prohibiting of compulsory attendance at Sunday Schools, and the use of sectarian tests for scholars. This latter revolution, for it is little less, was accomplished without the knowledge of Parliament by an ingenious juggle with the powers of the "South Kensington" and "Whitehall" Departments in the Evening School Code of 1901. It is thus seen by how many manoeuvres, obscure in themselves, but all parts of a consistent policy, the principle of popular control has been removed from a large field in which it had become established, and simultaneously the principle of clerical control has been extended, strengthened, and endowed.

THE FUTURE.

The Bills of 1900, 1901, and 1902, when studied with what is known of the objects of the Church Party in mind, will be seen to be designed to complete the work which has been so assiduously pursued. Immediately or ultimately School Boards, School Attendance Committees, and Technical Instruction Committees are to be abolished. New and limited functions are to be given to new authorities upon which Diocesan Associations and other clerical bodies are to have as large a representation as possible. The new authorities are to act in a large area, either the county or the diocese, their rating power is to be limited, and they are to give subsidies to existing schools, which are mainly clerical. The suggestion is made that these authorities shall not be allowed to provide schools under their own management, but even if this is not endorsed by Parliament, the statutory limit placed on their resources will bring about the desired result of preventing any large extension of educational facilities, and they are not to be subject to the statutory compulsion at present applied to School Boards, to provide adequate and efficient suitable education for all available scholars.

The clerical party has always taken the lead in Parliament against legislation or administration which insisted upon higher standards in buildings, in the curriculum, in the qualifications of teachers, and other educational requirements. This may be due to nothing more than indifference and lack of zeal for education, but when considered with this brief review of the reactionary policy of a century, it drives home the lesson that the forces against progress are focussed in the clerical party, which, with long views, able advocacy, enormous influence, and patient persistence, has so largely outflanked the principles of public management of national education.

CHAPTER III.—REFORM IN THE BOROUGHS.

THE educational provision of an average town is in the hands of four public authorities. In some boroughs there are more, in some less; but, few or many, the local authorities may nearly all be classified under the four following types :—(1) The School Board, elected and controlled by the ratepayers ; (2) the Managers of Voluntary Schools under the control of the Diocesan or other organisation ; (3) the Technical Education Committee, appointed by and under the control of the Town Council; (4) the Governors of Grammar Schools or similar institutions.

The evil of this division of labour is much misrepresented; there is talk of "competition," "overlapping," and "chaos." These are not the evils. The field of each authority is fairly well defined, and the Board of Education and the ratepayers between them have more effective powers to prevent wasteful competition than in most other departments of municipal work. The real evil of this system of "watertight compartments" is that the zeal, initiative, and adequate financial resources which accompany direct public management by the ratepayers are excluded from a large part of the work; that so far from "overlapping," harmful or beneficial, being general, there are frequently important public needs not supplied; that the great dividing lines prevent the co-ordination of the various institutions, and frequently present insurmountable barriers to the natural growth of popular education and the necessary progress of the individual scholar.

One Authority for All Grades.

It is almost common ground with all reformers that these "watertight compartments" should be thrown into one, and that in each town or city there shall be a single public authority supervising, controlling, and providing all grades of education. The problem is: Which of the existing models shall be copied in constituting the new authority? This is not a matter to be decided on personal grounds; there are many excellent men and women working in each section, and they can each show examples of most successful educational results. Local comparisons between this clergyman and that town councillor, this Board School and that Grammar School, are too narrow a basis upon which to decide great issues of popular education.

Local Option.

A most mischievous suggestion is, that the constitution of the new local education authority should be left to be decided by local option in each locality. Any one who has taken part in past struggles to persuade a locality to have a School Board, or a Technical Instruction Committee, or form a Voluntary School Association on popular lines, or adopt the Free Library Act, &c., knows the enormous power possessed by a small but well-organised vested interest to defeat the public need in such a contest, and can imagine what a patchwork of incongruous local bodies would be evolved from the turmoil. This is a question which calls for the highest powers of practised statesmanship. It must be decided by Parliament.

SUBSTITUTES FOR POPULAR CONTROL.

Parliament fully considered this matter in 1870, and after beginning with the idea of a Town Council Committee, decided in favour of direct election, just as in the same year, and later, it considered a variety of schemes for the indirect election of County Councils, but came at last, in 1888, to the principle of direct election. The two other types, Diocesan Association and Grammar School Governors, have never really been considered seriously by Parliament at all; they owe their existence to the administrative act of Government Departments. We know that the policy of the present Government, as revealed in their recent Bills, is opposed to both the School Board type and the Town Council Committee type; their scheme is a sort of combination of the Board of Governors of a Grammar School and the Diocesan Association. However, the public in most towns has before them the four types, and can judge which model should be adopted.

Most matters of local public concern are already controlled by well-established principles of local self-government which can be applied to education with just as much confidence as to other branches of municipal life. Judged by these principles, the Voluntary School model is condemned; for the public welfare has never been served by entrusting public work to individuals who have other interests to serve, and who are controlled, not by those who gain or suffer by their work, but by outside and distant organisations. If the clerical managers of the Clerical Schools were controlled by the parents and ratepayers, instead of by the Bishops and the Diocesan Association, the schools would be different. Judged also by these principles the typical Grammar School model is condemned. Partly composed of a few persons serving *ex-officio* because they hold high office in Church and State, partly nominated by select classes, such as the magistrates and University Senates, they frequently leave their responsibilities entirely in the hands of their officials; they are but slowly

responsive to popular wishes, often influenced by social traditions, and inclined to fix their ideals more on gathering scholars
from distant parts who will win greater renown for the school
in their charge than on educating the community under their
care. The School Board and the Town Council Technical
Instruction Committee, being subject to popular control, and
having the right to supplement their resources from the rates,
escape some of the defects of the others. The defects of the
Town Council Committee as at present constituted, such as
its limited resources, its freedom from any statutory obligation
to do anything, &c., have been already indicated. It is possible
to imagine these removed, and the reformer brought face to
face with the simple issue :—Other things being equal, is it
desirable that education should be entrusted to an independent
authority elected for the purpose, or should it be added to the
other functions of the Municipal Corporation?

DIRECT ELECTION FOR EDUCATION ONLY.

In theory there is much to be said for one public body
covering the whole field of local self-government, but in practice
some division is found to be desirable. Every public body
from the House of Commons downwards suffers by the enormous demands the duties make upon the members. The
prospect excludes many of the most suitable men. The
mingling of many issues in one election deprives the electors
of the effective decision of any one of them. The man who
would be willing to serve the community in one department is
embarrassed by being obliged to take his share of work and
responsibility in many others. These practical considerations
point to the need for a well-considered division of labour.
The lines of such division seem to have been found in the
present practice of having three directly-elected municipal
bodies in each municipal borough—one for poor law, one for
education, and one for roads, drains, gas, water, tramways, &c.
It is the almost universal experience that the work of either the
Town Council, the Board of Guardians, or the School Board is
as much as or more than one individual can grasp. Ambitious
men have occasionally tried to serve on all or on two, but have
generally failed. Arguments might be advanced for carrying

this division still further, as has been done with regard to education, as is done in some cases with regard to police, asylums, or licensing, and as is proposed with regard to water in London. This is eminently a question to be decided on practical grounds, with a clear idea of the advantages of complete unity on one hand, and of the advantages of a well-thought-out division of labour on the other. The present system of separate authorities for education, for poor relief, and for ordinary municipal work is well devised. The work of each is so distinct that it attracts different types of men; the work of each is so exacting, and requires such a long study of special principles and many statutes, that each is alone enough for any ordinary man. As regards education, it is especially necessary to have recurring appeals to the mass of the electorate on this issue alone in order to form any public opinion on such an intricate question, to overcome the opposition of powerfully vested interests, and to obtain the sanction of the ratepayers to the large expenditure. Continuity of policy down to technical details is most essential in school management, and if educational issues were mingled with others at the polls, the whole work might be imperilled by some change of public opinion on other matters. Direct election gives to the elected courage in facing necessary conflict, and elicits from the ratepayers their confidence and consequent subsidies for necessary expenditure. There is timidity, evasiveness, or sheer indifference in many of the indirectly elected bodies. In order to realise what potentiality of progress is embodied in the principle of direct election, take, as a single example, the foolish talk about the sectarian strife on School Boards. This comes from those who do not realise that the School Board is the only body which has "grasped this nettle," and in the course of one generation has cast out the evil spirit of sectarian proselytism from half the schools in the country. It has only to be remembered how this vital issue has been shirked in other countries, and by our own Parliament, and by governors of universities, colleges, and public schools, and by Technical Instruction Committees and School Attendance Committees, to realise that only a power directly derived from the people, and frequently refreshed by recurrent election contests, can grapple with the most potent reactionary force in the educational world.

THE PROGRESSIVE POLICY.

If Parliament is allowed to discuss the question fully, it must decide in favour of establishing in each town a single independent authority directly elected for the purposes of education, and taking cognisance of all grades of education. It is essential that this authority should take over from the School Board all its duties and all its statutory powers unimpaired. There should be no statutory limit on its rating power, and no statutory restriction on the ratepayers in their selection of members, subject to an effective obligation to provide suitable instruction for all scholars needing it. The new authority should also take over all the educational work of the Technical Instruction Committee and of the School Attendance Committee, and the distribution of the " Aid Grant " to Voluntary Schools now in the hands of diocesan and other authorities. Any Grammar School or similar institution maintained by public endowments should be transferred to it, and the scope of its labours should not be restricted by any statutory limitation of age or curriculum.

There is no startling novelty in the above suggestion. It is simply a practical amalgamation of powers which exist in most towns; and as for other places, there is nothing revolutionary in compelling a few backward towns (what one may call the " insanitary areas " of the educational field) to take up their due share of the national burden. If these proposals excite opposition, it is due to the fact that the air is at present full of reactionary schemes designed under cover of pretended reforms to curtail or destroy established principles of local self-government, and, instead of bringing the backward districts up to the general level, to throw back the best districts to the level of the worst.

POWER TO COMBINE.

One more essential principle is of great importance. This is the need for education authorities to be able to combine and act as one for any educational purpose. The duties of an Education Authority include many grades of work, and different grades are more or less effectively performed over larger or smaller areas. Thus a very small population will support an ordinary Elementary School; but a larger population is required for a Secondary School, a larger for an Industrial School, a larger for a Teachers' Training College, a larger for a University College. It is obvious that although the accepted area for municipal self-government must be the unit of administration, each unit must be able to join forces with one or more other units for any purpose which is too large for one singly. This is most successfully accomplished by School Boards under the Act of 1870; adjoining Boards unite to establish a common centre for training pupil teachers, or blind or deaf children, distant ones (for instance, London and Brighton) uniting to establish an Industrial School. If School Boards had been given similar powers to join in establishing Training Colleges for teachers, the long-existing deficiency of trained teachers would have been supplied.

CHAPTER IV.—REFORM IN THE COUNTIES.

THERE is a too common impression that local self-government in the counties is administered by the County Councils. That is a mistake. The County Councils have general administrative duties in matters which are of common interest to the whole county, but local affairs are in the hands of local municipal councils.[1]

NON-COUNTY BOROUGHS AND OTHER TOWNS.

There is a too common impression that the county population, outside the sixty-seven towns which are "county boroughs," is rural and agricultural. That is a mistake. The greater part of the population of the counties (11,379,322) live in municipal boroughs, towns, and urban districts which have nearly all the characteristics of the county boroughs. Their population is sometimes as large, their public spirit as great, and in many of the municipal boroughs their possession of local self-government more ancient.

No reason exists for making any distinction in educational matters between these urban districts and the county boroughs.

[1] For municipal purposes the country outside London is divided into 1,121 "urban districts" and 606 "rural districts." Sixty-seven of the urban districts are county boroughs.

Both classes are well qualified for local independence in local matters, and if they join others in enterprises which require more than a strictly local sphere of operation, they need to join on equal terms.

THE VILLAGES.

The remainder of the county population (7,471,242) resides in the rural villages. Much is said in condemnation of the villages from an educational point of view. Let us leave that issue for a moment to consider the larger question of the general organisation for other municipal matters. The persons who hate all democratic self-government are never tired of reminding us that villages with an average population of five hundred or six hundred cannot maintain individually the same local system of municipal government as the big towns. This is equally true of the separate parishes and wards of a city. Just as these latter are united into one effective municipality, sometimes large and sometimes small, so the wisdom of Parliament has endeavoured to group and unite the rural parishes for all except exclusively parochial purposes.

THE RURAL MUNICIPALITIES.

The first effort in this direction in modern times was the union of parishes for poor law purposes in 1834. As years passed on other groupings were made for other purposes, until the Local Government Act of 1894 took the growing chaos in hand, and amalgamated and reconstituted these local groups formed for different purposes into a universal system of one simple group for all purposes, and gave them the name of "county districts." There are 606 county districts governed by "Rural District Councils," formed by the union of from twenty to thirty rural parishes. These Districts are the real municipalities of the agricultural community; their boundaries have been carefully adjusted, their average population and rateable value are as large as those of the average municipal borough, their councils are endowed with nearly all the powers of self-government of the Town Councils; and with the example of the boroughs before them they are destined to develop a full municipal life more rapidly than did the boroughs after the great Act of 1835.

Local Self-Government.

We thus find that the whole area of each county is divided into suitable municipal areas constituted with an eye to local conveniency, local rating, the organisation of local patriotism, and the general efficiency of local self-government. Every inch of the country is under a municipal authority for municipal purposes—either a Town Council, an Urban District Council, or a Rural District Council. Each district is large enough to include in its population persons of the class from which county councillors are drawn, as well as many others who cannot travel regularly to the county town to take part in county business, but are well qualified to conduct the affairs of their immediate district. If a few of them seem to be rather small for independent local self-government, we may rest assured that there are special local reasons for such a small area having been adopted.

The Small School Boards.

Now, let us glance at the educational affairs of these many towns and villages. Where there are no School Boards they are under "School Attendance Committees" appointed by the Urban or Rural District Councils, and these are often as ineffective as are those in the county boroughs. They suffer from the same defects, and are sometimes better, sometimes worse. Then the boroughs and urban districts have the same powers with regard to technical education as the county boroughs; they rival, and not infrequently excel them in public spirit; the heaviest self-imposed burden of rates for this purpose is to be found in these small towns. Hundreds of the towns and urban districts also have School Boards on exactly the same terms as the large cities; but in the rural districts the area appointed by Parliament for the election of a School Board is not the rural "county district" but the parish.

The Ecclesiastical Area.

Now, it is remarkable that the Act of 1870 should have fixed the parish as the unit of educational administration, because nearly every proposal for legislation before 1870 prescribed a larger area than the parish in the country as well as in the town. The truth is, that the parish is an ecclesiastical area as well as a civil area, and long before 1870 there had been frequent trouble and jealousy between the clergy of neighbouring parishes, when the children over whom they claimed jurisdiction attended a school which did not belong to either one parish or the other exclusively. In shaping the Bill of 1870 the influence of the ecclesiastics prevailed and the ecclesiastical area was adopted as the unit of administration. It was seen that such small areas might lead to inefficiency in some districts, but Mr Forster disarmed criticism by giving the Education Department ample powers to group any number of parishes together before forming a School Board, and he promised the House of Commons that this power should be freely used. The Board of Education therefore has power to unite the parishes of a whole district, or even a whole county, or even of all England and Wales under a single School Board, and if any of the present Rural School Boards are too small, it is the fault of the Board of Education which made them. The Board could enlarge them up to any suitable size to-morrow.

The Result of Popular Control.

But as the small size of many Rural School Boards is being used to discredit the whole system, let us examine the alleged defects. It must first be noted that the defects of a Village School Board are not the defects of the School Board, but the defects of the village. If the electors are few and timid, if the public men of a village are of a poor quality, local self-government may not be carried on with quite as much dignity and public spirit as in more fortunate places, it will not make that parish better to deprive it of local self-government. You must always work with the best material available, and the recurring election provides regular opportunities to improve it. Then, School Boards are, at present, comparatively rare, the Act made their establishment optional, and they have as a rule only been allowed to come into existence where all other means have failed. It would not be fair to judge the self-governing power of all rural districts by those few parishes in which School Boards have been established. But despite all this, some of the small School Boards are as good as the best big ones, and there is scarcely a village in the land under a School Board which is not in a better educational position to-day than

London, Liverpool, Birmingham, and other great cities were thirty years ago. If the poorest and most unfortunate parish lags only thirty years behind the greatest cities in the empire, it is worse than ridiculous to cover it with contumely. A more reasonable comparison is that between the villages in which education is under popular control and the villages in which education is under clerical control. An examination of the Government returns on these lines shows that by every available test of public spirit, self-sacrifice, and efficiency, the advantage is then with the village which has a School Board.

DISTRICT COUNCIL AREAS.

It has, however, been already stated that there are advantages to be gained by larger areas. It makes for good and economical administration when a Board has several schools under its care instead of only one. The difficulty in uniting parishes to form substantial areas has arisen mainly from the fact that the School Board system is optional, and that by refusing to unite, a parish may avoid its educational responsibilities. If Parliament decreed that there should be School Boards everywhere, the parishes would hasten to unite together into the most efficient and economical combinations. It is, however, an advantage to use the adopted municipal area for all municipal purposes, and the accepted municipal area in the rural districts is that of the Rural District Council. If the Rural School Board areas were coterminous with the Rural District Council areas, these education authorities would have an average of from fifteen to twenty schools in their districts, and a population larger than half of the municipal boroughs. Under authorities acting in such areas, all the petty criticism of small Boards would disappear. From such a population we might hope to enlist a local patriotism which would place rural education on a level with that of the towns. Higher elementary schools, evening continuation schools, central schools for pupil teachers and for industrial subjects would grow up in each one, as they have grown up in the towns.

THE FUNCTION OF A COUNTY AUTHORITY.

Enough has been said to show that there is no fundamental difference between the problems of reform and progress in county boroughs and in towns and villages which are not county boroughs. They all need a genuine local authority with similar powers, duties, obligations, and constitution, established in the accepted areas of local municipal self-government. No doubt amongst these smaller towns and rural districts there is more need for that power of uniting for joint action upon which stress has been laid in discussing the case of the county boroughs. Authorities which only provide for a population of 20,000 or 30,000, whether in a single town or a group of villages, are less able to provide singly some of the educational institutions needing a large area in which to operate, and the power of combination, if granted, would be more freely used. The business of organising suitable combinations of local education authorities for each purpose, and joining them into large or small organisations with the big boroughs for such purposes as a great Secondary School, a Technical Institute or Teachers' Training College or a Provincial University would be important. It might well be initiated by the County Council. The guiding principle as to where a line should be drawn between the function of a local education authority and of the County Council being that no locality should be dependent on the consent of other localities for its exclusively local supply of education; for to subject the desires of one locality to the self-interested veto of other districts is the greatest hindrance to progress. This reactionary force is not altogether unknown amongst the various parishes or wards of a great city, whose interests are nevertheless most obviously one and indivisible: it is naturally potent in an area as wide as an ordinary county. On the other hand, experience shows that people who object to be rated for the education of some remote and unknown district will under the influence of local patriotism gladly rate themselves heavily for the benefit of their own.

A REACTIONARY POLICY.

The policy put forward by the Government of taking all education out of the hands of the non-county boroughs, the towns, and the rural districts, and placing it in the hands of an authority, organised in a wider area, is a reactionary policy. To give a power of vetoing local effort and suppressing local patriotism would never do good and would often do harm. This is especially true in such a matter as popular education. The fundamental facts of educational progress are that all really successful educational work of all grades must be built upon a well-managed elementary school, and that the area and constitution of a local education authority should be fixed with special regard to the efficient management of elementary schools. Let this be secured, and all the rest will follow naturally if adequate machinery for combined effort is provided. To place all village schools under an authority acting in an area as large as a county or a diocese, even if that authority were directly elected, would only be giving the form of self-government and withholding the substance. There are in each county hundreds of villages, they each need special treatment and a determined local public opinion. How can this be obtained through a county organisation? The average village has one-tenth share in one County Councillor, he is about one-fiftieth of the Council; it is suggested that the Council should appoint one-half of a county education authority, the county authority would nominate District Committees, the District Committees would nominate Sub-Committees, and the Sub-Committees appoint some one to manage the village school if a public school, and one-third of the managers if a sectarian school! By the time whatever local public opinion on the education question elicited at the election of the County Councillor had filtered through all these intermediate Committees, there would not be an ounce of local public opinion to a ton of something else operating in the management of the local school.

This is a very Tory clerical theory of local self-government. It reinstates a despotism, under a form of popular election, for the managers would be absolutely beyond any sense of responsibility to local public opinion. The only real popular control is that which places the school under the absolute management of persons directly elected by those who have to gain or suffer by the way it is managed.

CHAPTER V.—VESTED INTERESTS.

THE greatest practical difficulty in making any constructive reform is the antagonism of vested interests. It is not only the policy of the British Parliament but a striking characteristic of the British people to be tender and generous to every vested interest. But it is the inherent defect of all vested interests to be selfish, to meet troubles more than half-way, to be sensitive to the verge of cowardice, and to fight unnecessarily and unscrupulously. To take one simple illustration. Before establishing Board Schools, Parliament amply and generously safeguarded the interests of Voluntary Schools. This did not prevent the Voluntary Schools filling the air for thirty years with clamorous outcries that the Board Schools would kill them; but at the end of thirty years, owing solely to the monopoly and preferential claim given them by the Government in the Act of 1870, and by subsequent legislation and administration, the Voluntary Schools are not diminished, but are increased a hundred per cent. How often also have the universities, the endowed schools, and the private schools been benefited by reforms which they had blindly and fiercely resisted?

Public Provision and Private Provision.

How to meet and how to deal with the vested interests still remains the greatest problem in the reform of national education. The first principle to be grasped is that the creation of a national system does not necessarily mean the extinction of all other provision. Public libraries do not extinguish private libraries, nor public parks abolish private gardens, nor public baths abolish private baths, nor public tramways extinguish hansom cabs or private carriages; on the contrary, there is ample evidence that the public provision, however great, still creates a greater demand and stimulates a general taste, habit, and desire, by which other agencies are benefited. Therefore it is of first importance to remember that other agencies can and will flourish side by side with a national system, and that it is not necessary either to suppress or injure other agencies before setting up a national system.

The Vested Interests.

Now the three great classes of vested interests which are actively opposing the establishment of a complete system of national education are—(1) The endowed schools; (2) the denominational schools; and (3) the private schools.

The endowed schools are in a different position from the others. Some temporary personal interests might have to be considered if any sudden change were made in their management, but, broadly, they are dedicated to the cause of national education and nothing else. They are supported by endowments which are virtually public property, they are under a sort of public control, and there is no separate interest to be considered. They may be dealt with in any way which seems to be wise and in the public interest without any injustice being done.

The denominational schools, elementary and secondary, are differently situated. They are more or less the private property of religious organisations, and are maintained primarily for sectarian purposes.

The private schools also have been provided by private capital, and are maintained more or less as private commercial undertakings, and their proprietors are entitled to all the protection granted to other traders when affected by a change in public policy.

THE RIGHTS AND DUTIES OF THE NATION.

None of these agencies has a monopoly, they are always liable to every kind of competition, and they have not the shadow of a claim to prevent the nation or the municipality from competing with them. Therefore any compromise or compensation which the State may make is a matter of favour and not comparable with arrangements made when any right or property is confiscated.

The position is: that the State has an imperative duty to secure for all its citizens an adequate provision of efficient and suitable education and that these private and sectarian institutions, dreading possible competition, come forward and ask to be accepted as part of that provision. The State has to consider whether it will recognise and accept these schools or refuse to do so.

Meanwhile the fundamental right of the State is negatived by active political obstruction organised by the vested interests, and before the State can perform its duties it must make terms with the obstructors.

THE SETTLEMENT OF 1870.

With regard to the denominational schools, what was the settlement made in 1870? It was that if a school (1) reached a certain minimum of efficiency; (2) allowed scholars of other creeds to attend without attempting to proselytise them; (3) was housed in adequate buildings; and (4) obtained half the income necessary for maintenance from local sources; then the State agreed that it should be recognised as suitable, be free from competition, and be subsidised by a grant not exceeding the local contribution. If any school failed in any of these matters, the State was to withdraw its recognition and take steps to provide a school under public control. The bargain was generous, too generous, but it has never been kept by the denominational schools. The conditions of efficiency have been resisted and defied, the stipulated share of the cost has seldom been provided, the rights of conscience have been disregarded, and the buildings have been inadequate. It is obviously the duty of the State to enforce strictly the terms of the settlement on these points. And the moral obligation still lying on the denominational school to fulfil the terms of the old settlement ought to be considered in any new arrangement.

COMPULSION AND A CHOICE OF SCHOOLS.

Another point has arisen. In 1870 no one was compelled to attend these schools. Much stress was laid upon the fact that the necessity of attracting scholars must be the greatest safeguard for efficiency and fair management. If a school were in any way unsatisfactory, the scholars would not attend and the school would be ruined. This safeguard has disappeared since 1870. Compulsory attendance under pain of fine and imprisonment has been introduced. The scholars are driven to the denominational schools. They have no option but to attend, they have practically no choice of schools, and the safeguard for efficiency and suitability upon which so much stress was laid in 1870 has disappeared. The first duty of the State is to restore to the parents the choice of schools which was part of the settlement of 1870. If any section of the community does not wish for denominational schools the public authority must be allowed, and should be not only allowed but compelled, to provide schools under public management for all who prefer them. And the public authority drawing money from all denominations should have no power to provide exclusive denominational schools for the benefit of one.

PUBLIC MONEY IN PRIVATE HANDS.

Then there is the question of giving grants. And here the only clear principle is that it is absolutely unsound and wasteful to give subsidies to private enterprises, and that the expenditure of all public money should be under public management. Religious organisations or private individuals may establish whatever schools they think well and teach whatever they like, at their own expense, and no one proposes to prevent them. When they ask for public money the conditions wholly change. A system of giving grants-in-aid to such schools has grown up, however, and will probably continue. The whole principle is pernicious, but if grants are demanded it is necessary to consider what conditions shall be attached to the grant.

DENOMINATIONAL SCHOOLS NOT NEEDED BY THE STATE.

The first salient fact to realise in considering this point is that since 1870 the State has not been dependent upon these schools for the supply of education. If any one of them closes its doors it is immediately replaced. Before 1870 the schools provided by private or sectarian effort were the only provision. If any private or sectarian school closed its doors an injury was done to the cause of national education. A section of the community was left without the means of elementary instruction. The State was accordingly obliged to subsidise these schools, to nurse them and almost to maintain them if it wished to see education extended. Since 1870 all that has changed. The closing of a denominational school now is more often than not a direct and immediate benefit. The great bulk of them are merely standing in the way of the immediate establishment of something better.

THE STATE OWES THEM NOTHING.

Then the State owes them nothing. There is not even a moral debt. Day by day they do the State some service in educating certain scholars, and day by day they obtain their reward. They receive the Government grants. They manage the school, they appoint the teachers, and they prosecute a sectarian propaganda as part of the curriculum. But it is claimed that they have provided permanent buildings. It is true, but they have not given the buildings to the public.

They have built buildings, and they keep them. These premises have been built partly and often primarily for ecclesiastical purposes. They are required for Sunday schools, for church meetings, and for similar work. By allowing them to be also occupied by a day school the denomination secured towards their erection public grants and public subscriptions which would not have been given for purely denominational purposes. Moreover, if the buildings belong to the denomination, the State can hire them or purchase them on such terms as will fully repay any unexhausted value on that account. Therefore as matters stand at present, there is no need or reason whatever why the State should help to continue the existence of these schools if they are not desired by the community. If their proprietors desire to continue them, they may equitably be called upon to maintain them at their own cost from the day the local community decides to establish schools of its own. If any of them cease to exist, the public need would still be supplied.

An Equitable Claim.

The logical conclusion of this last argument cannot always be reached, because it is not in the public interest that there shall be competing schools, especially in districts such as rural villages, where the population is only sufficient to fill one school effectively, and as the law stands at present the existing schools have a certain monopoly secured to them. If, therefore, in the completion of a national system the Education Authorities are empowered to establish new schools which might compete with any existing schools, either public or private, it would be wise to give the proprietors of any existing school a right to call on the public authority to take it over on equitable terms.

Buildings.

In considering terms of transfer it is desirable to distinguish clearly between the school and the building in which the school is conducted. The use of the word "school" to denote either a building or the institution which meets under its roof leads to endless confusion. A "school," like any business, corporation, society, or other organisation, is entirely separable from the "schoolhouse" in which its affairs are transacted. In commercial language, there are the "goodwill" and the "premises." Each has a value distinct from the other, and either may be transferred without the other. Now in considering the transfer of a "school" and of a "schoolhouse," the latter has a capital value, easily ascertainable, and, if called upon to do so, the Education Authority might take it over and pay for it on fair commercial terms. Of course if the building were held in trust the proceeds would have to be applied in accordance with the terms of the trust deed or as the law relating to such matters directs.

GOODWILL.

Then to the proprietor, who is conducting a school for the financial profit it brings, his "goodwill," as apart from the mere building, is an ascertainable financial sum, and there is no reason why that should not be paid. But to the religious organisation conducting a school as part of a sectarian propaganda, the value of the "school," as distinct from the premises, cannot be measured in terms of money. It consists mainly in the right to appoint the teachers of a certain number of scholars, to give denominational teaching to those who do not refuse to receive it, and generally to influence them in favour of a particular denomination. This is the privilege which is so fiercely defended.

DENOMINATIONAL PRIVILEGES.

So far as this sectarian domination is exercised by members of one religious denomination over members of another, it is offensive and intolerable, and should be promptly abrogated without compensation or consideration. So far as it is merely exercised by the authorities of one denomination over their own adherents, it is well to remember that there are many other opportunities for giving sectarian teaching and influencing the people in favour of a particular denomination, that the nation supports schools for national and not for sectarian purposes, that scholars only attend school during four or five hours a day on five days in the week, or, roughly, one hour in eight, and that sectarian zeal might well spare the children for the one hour, and be content to ply its propaganda in the other seven ; or if it considers it must mingle theology with the school curriculum, then it can provide schools at its own expense for the purpose.

Terms of Settlement.

But the sectarian monopoly exists in schools which it may be necessary to transfer from private management to public management. Practical statesmanship has to consider what terms can be offered to make the transfer acceptable. First, it is feasible to give to a church the free use of a building outside the hours of compulsory attendance, for any teaching, services, or other purposes which do not interfere with the work of the school. Secondly, it is possible to appoint members of the existing governing body of a school as managers of the school when it has been transferred to the Education Authority. The Act of 1870 (Section 15) provides for a School Board delegating any of their powers, except the power of raising money, to a body of managers appointed by the Board. By this means all the power they at present possess, which is not antagonistic to the public interest, might be continued to the proprietors of a transferred school. If any concessions of this kind were entertained it would have to be remembered that the circumstances of each school differ so much that there must be a separate negotiation in each case. As a special safeguard for private interests, the terms suggested might be made part of an agreement of transfer which would not be valid unless sanctioned by the Board of Education.

Unfounded Fears.

By such measures as these the efficiency of all schools could be secured, and all private interests deserving consideration could be fully safeguarded. The whole experience of public life in England shows that fears of injustice or hardship are quite unfounded. Whenever a vested interest is dealt with either by Parliament or by a public department it always gets the best of the bargain; even the most injurious monopoly, whilst meeting with strenuous opposition to any extension of its power, will be treated with liberality when its powers are curtailed. The dislike of democratic influences that inspires the existing vested interests is based on a misreading of history, and, so far as they have any desire to promote the public welfare, they degrade themselves by opposing the creation of a complete national system of public education.

CHAPTER VI.—FINANCIAL PROBLEMS.

THE education question is pre-eminently one of finance. It is also pre-eminently one in which all financial principles have been thrown to the winds. It is only in comparatively recent years that rates and taxes have been drawn upon. The present arrangement of rates and taxes are so unsound that the nation bears an enormous financial burden, and does not get value for its money.

FEES.

There are people who argue that education should be paid for by the scholar, and grow eloquent upon the iniquity of providing free education for the people. They forget that it is hardly an exaggeration to say that in almost all ages and all countries it has never been found possible to extract from the scholars of any class of society, fees equal to the cost of their education. Even in wealthy England to-day in the Universities, the great public schools, or even many of the institutions which are apparently maintained on a commercial basis, few students pay the full cost of their education. And amongst the mass of the people if fees are low they are inadequate, and if high, they restrict the diffusion of knowledge.

ENDOWMENTS.

The historic basis of educational finance is an endowment by "pious founders." But endowments have throughout the ages proved demoralising and wasteful. An endowment breeds stagnation and brings the smallest possible return for expenditure. It involves a strict trust deed and the consequent tyranny of the "dead hand" controlling a process which, if it is to be efficient, should be guided by ideals for the future rather than traditions of the past. Probably nothing has so injured national education as some of the endowments intended to promote it.

VOLUNTARY SUBSCRIPTIONS.

The living money of the living generations is the only trustworthy resource. For many generations, in all grades of education, all kinds of disinterested or self-interested contributors of voluntary subscriptions have gallantly struggled to fill the educational treasury. But the voluntary principle is unreliable. It has always proved inadequate for any requirements on a large scale; it often fails for lack of that proper organisation which inspires confidence and cheerful giving.

RATES AND TAXES.

After all a democratic system of rating and taxing is nothing but a properly organised method of voluntary subscription. The "bottomless purse" of the ratepayers and the taxpayers is a fallacy. The bottom is reached as soon as it is opened unless the ratepayers and taxpayers give their confidence and consent to those who are entrusted with the expenditure of their money. Nothing is more noteworthy in the present position of affairs than the fact that people who will not subscribe to private organisation readily pay a rate to a duly constituted authority; or that an authority constituted on an undemocratic basis dare not and cannot levy a penny rate whilst the ratepayers readily yield a rate of two or three shillings to an authority which they directly elect and control, and are proud of it.

DOLES.

Nothing is so easily wasted as public money if not disbursed under proper safeguards. Again and again a temporary majority in Parliament has flung large doles of public money to its friends beyond hope of recovery. The history of educational finance shows a long series of discreditable raids on the National Exchequer. The much abused code of Mr Lowe was rendered necessary by half a century of fruitless doles which were producing a most inadequate result. That had been a period of open denominational endowment under a thin veil of educational provision. After 1870 the process had to be more subtle. The Free Education Act was an ingenious device to give a large dole to denominational schools under the guise of a popular reform. For years the ratepayers of many districts had only asked to be allowed to abolish fees and fill the gap from the rates. The *average* fees for the whole country worked out at about 3d. per week per child. The Government gave a uniform grant of this amount in return for the abolition of fees under and up to this sum. The total sum now paid is over £2,000,000 per annum. The schools charging a fee below the average received much more than they surrendered, and those which charged a higher fee were allowed to take the grant and still charge the balance. It was a dole to the worst schools, and the Marquis of Salisbury boasted of it.

In 1899 the ordinary educational grant was manipulated in the same way. An equal grant to all schools given practically without regard to efficiency, effort, or need, did incalculable harm by cutting off about £30,000 from the best schools (a trifling sum to the Exchequer which was working wonders in stimulating every ambitious school to greater effort), and at the same time about £250,000 was drawn automatically from the Exchequer for the worst schools which were neglecting their duty.

In 1897 under the plea of poverty the "aid grant" was asked for, and the Chancellor of the Exchequer was induced to give a grant of over £600,000 per annum and leave it to Diocesan and other associations to distribute. They have frequently used it as a "fighting fund" to just keep the worst schools alive and keep all schools struggling, instead of making those schools really efficient which could be made efficient, and leaving the rest to be replaced by efficient Board Schools.

In 1889 a sum now amounting to nearly £800,000 per annum was voted by Parliament to buy up public-houses as part of a scheme of licensing reform, the Bill allocating the money was withdrawn, but the money had been voted for the year, and in subsequent years the grant was continued in the understanding that it should be used for technical education. But no guarantees were taken that it should be so spent or wisely spent. Much of it has gone in the relief of ordinary rates, much of it in sectarian endowment, and much of it has been wasted.

The result of all these doles is that the national treasury is the poorer by many millions, and education is but poorly benefited. They are a sad object-lesson for a distracted Chancellor of the Exchequer.

SOUND PRINCIPLES.

Grants in aid may be given liberally from the national treasury if they are given on conditions which stimulate local effort and rise and fall in proportion with it. If they give the local authority twopence or even sixpence for each penny it provides, the joint fund will probably be wisely spent. For it is the principle of our system of local self-government to secure economy by securing the vigilant control of those who feel some burden of the cost, and to secure an adequate expenditure by giving power to those who will benefit by it. It is only when a community feels that it is spending its own money for its own benefit that it is wisely liberal and wisely thrifty.

Nearly fifty years ago, the present Archbishop of Canterbury uttered a solemn warning against the reckless increase of the Parliamentary grant which was even then in progress. He said :—

"The plain issue to all this is and can be nothing but to place the entire burden on the central revenue. Then follow all the evils of centralisation—waste by the local authorities, tyranny by the central. The local authorities, deprived of that spur to vigilant economy on which alone any ultimate reliance can be placed, namely, the sense that they are dealing with their own money, slip gradually into waste which no supervision can prevent. The central authority struggles to guard its trust by rules which are right on the whole, but tyrannical in detail, and dares not relax those rules when they ought to be relaxed, because experience proves to demonstration that one justifiable relaxation inevitably admits a hundred unjustifiable."
—*Oxford Essays* (1856), p. 270.

Succeeding years have shown how true this warning was.

Education is primarily a local benefit, and should be primarily a local charge. National aid should supplement and not supplant, should stimulate and not stifle.

GLADSTONIAN FINANCE.

Only once has Parliament fairly faced the problem of finance in national education. This was in 1870. The Parliamentary grant was largely increased, but it was put on sound principles. It was then arranged that in future the ordinary grant should not be given until local resources had provided a certain efficient minimum of buildings, staff and teaching. Then grants were offered in such a way as to stimulate further efficiency. But for every penny provided by the Government a penny had to be provided by the locality. This fundamental basis being established, the obvious difficulty that some districts are rich and others poor was met by an ingenious sliding-scale arrangement intended to secure that in poor districts all expenditure above the normal should be provided by a special additional grant. Thus the poorer districts would have a handsome subsidy, and practically the rate would be equalised over the whole country, wherever local effort and local sacrifice were equal. Unfortunately, there was a serious miscalculation in devising the scale, and it has only a limited application, but the principle is sound, and if properly applied would do ten times more for efficient education, at a tenth of the cost, than some of the reckless doles which succeeding Chancellors of the Exchequer have recklessly given.

Doles again.

Since 1870 Parliament has never given serious thought to the principles of finance in education. The clergy have clamoured for doles, and have clamoured to be relieved from any obligation to find money, or to make their schools efficient. Bit by bit every safeguard has disappeared, and at the same time money has been poured out like water. The national subsidy for the maintenance of elementary schools was in 1870 about £650,000; in 1900 it was £8,220,000. In 1870 the locality provided 62 per cent. of the cost; in 1900 the locality found for voluntary schools 33 per cent., and for Board schools 41 per cent. Before 1876 every separate penny of a grant brought automatically some corresponding local contribution and some increase of efficiency. In 1902, beyond the vaguest threat that the whole grant may be withheld, there is no safeguard for either.

Debtors to the Nation.

Now let us try to estimate what the financial position would be if a patriotic Chancellor of the Exchequer were once more to enforce the principles of 1870. The present annual expenditure from all sources on elementary education (apart from capital expenditure on buildings) is roughly £13,000,000, of which the National Exchequer provides £8,000,000. If, as agreed in 1870, the National Exchequer provided only half the cost, there would be a windfall for the National Exchequer of £1,500,000 per annum. Many towns and parishes (containing about one-third of the population) have evaded the education rate, prescribed in 1870, mainly by cursing the country with poor and inefficient schools. They have escaped an obvious duty for thirty years. It is time they were compelled to assume their fair share of the burden of national education. The average rate in School Board districts is 9d. in the pound, and if the districts which have never paid a rate were to be rated on this basis it would produce an additional contribution for national education of nearly £2,000,000 per annum.

Or, if the subscribers to voluntary schools (largely big railway companies and other rich people trying to avoid a rate) fulfilled their bargain of 1870, and obtained from local sources half the cost of the present maintenance of their schools, this would produce £1,750,000 per annum.

If the Chancellor of the Exchequer is thinking about safeguarding the National Exchequer, here are two debtors who have, to the great detriment of education, evaded their just debts. They are deserving of no consideration from the other portions of the community which, already burdened with their own rates, have also, as taxpayers, been largely bearing the burden of these defaulters.

The places which have avoided a School Board rate are mainly such places as Wimbledon, Surbiton, Ealing, Twickenham, and other wealthy districts in the Thames Valley; or Stockport, Preston, Accrington, and other prosperous boroughs in Lancashire.

The defaulting ratepayer and defaulting subscriber, who evade their financial obligations and burden the country with bad and inefficient schools, are, to a certain extent, identical; but their total obligation in rates or subscriptions cannot be less than £2,000,000 per annum.

Then there are the county and urban councils who have been entrusted with educational duties which they have not always performed. They were empowered in 1889 to levy a penny rate, and have seldom done so. They owe about £1,000,000 per annum.

THE DUTY OF THE CHANCELLOR OF THE EXCHEQUER.

There is thus a total of about £3,000,000 per annum lying dormant. Money which has long been due, but which will never be provided by the debtors so long as Parliament weakly overlooks their neglect and the Chancellor of the Exchequer weakly allows them, whenever they are pressed for funds, to draw at sight on the National Treasury.

If the National Exchequer were relieved of the burden of supplying this deficiency, the sliding-scale of 1870 might be adjusted so as to give a special grant in aid to the poor districts. The normal education rate would then be reduced to about 6d. in the pound, without any addition to the drain on the Exchequer. The heavy burden on the ratepayers in some districts is largely due to the fact that other districts pay no education rate at all. Let each part of the country bear its equal share of rates, and the local burden would be lighter and the national burden no heavier.

It ought to fill the Chancellor of the Exchequer with remorse to see how readily some towns and villages bear a burden of a 1s. or 2s. rate for education and are proud of it, whilst he has meekly allowed a few big ratepayers of other towns and villages to force him to find the money to meet their local obligations, especially if he realises that this is only the action of a few influential people, and that the mass of the electorate was ready and willing to bear its burden if only it were allowed to take the education of the district into its own hands at its own expense.

THE NEW DEMANDS.

The clerical party are once more crying, "Give, give." The answer is ready :—" Your difficulties have nothing to do with the National Exchequer, and you have no need for any change in the law before the school is aided by the rates. Either find the money by the voluntary contributions of the richest church in the world, or hand any school which is in difficulties over to a School Board, in accordance with the Act of 1870. Let it be managed by the local ratepayers, the majority of whom are willing to make it efficient at the public expense, provided that they also have the management. And do not imagine that you will obtain relief by a new law enabling the ratepayers to give you money without taking also the management of the school. For the ratepayers cannot be compelled to levy rates, even when they have the power, and their purse is generally tightly closed unless they are going to spend their money on their own property, for their own benefit, under their own management and control."

www.ingramcontent.com/pod-product-compliance
Lightning Source LLC
Chambersburg PA
CBHW081304040426
42452CB00014B/2643